PRETTY GIRLS PRAY

DR. TAMARRAH TARVER

Copyright © 2015 Tamarrah Tarver

Printed in the United States of America

ISBN: 978-0-692-53604-9

DEDICATION

To my son Christopher,

You are my lifeline. I know what agape love is because of you. The day that I gave birth to you, was the most life changing and amazing day of my life. May I model a life that is both encouraging and enhancing to your life. I love you more than words could ever express. Mommy dedicates this book to you, for you are an answer to a prayer that I prayed over 10 years ago! I'm thankful that God answered that prayer when he blessed me with you. I love you Christopher!

CONTENTS

ACKNOWLEDGMENTS

To the Creator, thank you for life. I am because you are. I honor you above all.

I would like to express thanks and gratitude to some incredible people that assisted in the production of this book.

To my parents, Willie and Karen Powell. Thank you for the sacrifices that you have made for me. I am beyond blessed to have parents like you.

To my biological father, Stanley Tarver, RIP. I hope that I am making you smile.

To my grandparents, Robert and Cathy Smith, thanks for your unending love and support. Your prayers are the reason I am here today.

To my siblings, Ashlee, Jervon, and Danielle, thanks for believing in your big sister. I am beyond thankful to have you as my blood siblings.

To "The Pretty Team," thanks for riding with me on this entrepreneurial journey. I appreciate you hard word towards the PGW vision.

To my friends, relatives, mentors, and acquaintances, thank you for believing in me. Your support is appreciated.

TO YOU, THE READER, THANK YOU FOR YOUR WILLINGNESS TO GROW SPIRITUALLY IN PRAYER. I APPRECIATE YOU.

CHAPTER 1: PRAYER

What is prayer?

Simply expressed, prayer is dialogue with God. It's talking and communicating with God. You speak to God and he speaks back to you. In essence, it is the intimate conversation that one has with the creator, God. It is one of the many currencies of Heaven.

Prayer is the best wireless connection that one can have. Pretty Girl, it's better than Sprint, T mobile, and Verizon. You will never have to worry about a bad connection, because you will be able to reach the source of the connection, GOD. Prayer is rejuvenation to the spirit of man. It awakens the human consciousness. Metaphorically speaking, prayer is spiritual breathing. Prayer gives oxygen and life to the soul and spirit. The most important and vital conversation that you will have on any given day, is the conversation that you have with God. It is the key ingredient for a healthy spiritual life. In your interpersonal relationships, you can't sustain those relationships without effective and consistent communication. The more that you converse with others, the more intimate you become with them, and the more you understand who they are. This is synonymous with your communication with God. The more that you communicate with him, the more you will understand his likes, dislikes, approval, and disapproval of your life. You will also begin to understand the mind of God as your prayer life deepens. A key component to prayer is quieting your spirit. When you settle and quiet your spirit, you can hear God clearly, devoid of distractions. This means removing yourself from watching television, checking social media, idle chatter on the telephone, and disengaging from all forms of distractions during your time in prayer. This is a time that should be devoted to God. I hope you have a better understanding of prayer.

Do you remember when you were in grade school and you read a text and the teacher asked you the 5 W's and 1 H? This was the Who? What? When? Where? Why? and How? of the text. Let's embark upon the 5 W's and 1 H of prayer.

Who should pray?

God created man and woman. We all possess the DNA of the Creator. However, we have been given free will to choose to pray or not to pray. Prayer is a choice. EVERYONE should pray. If you understand basic rhetoric, you should pray. This includes man, woman, boy, and girl!

What to pray?

There are a plethora of people, circumstances, and things to pray for. Each person must be in tune with the frequency of Heaven, to understand what to pray for.

Here's a few examples of what you can pray for.

- Pray for yourself. Pray to have the fruit of the spirit.

- Pray for your church. Pray for your leaders and the local body of believers.

  a) Pray for your family. Pray for unity in your familial bloodline. Pray for their homes, health, and finances.

- Pray for the government. Pray that God's wisdom would migrate to the judicial system's infrastructure.

- Pray for the Nation. The Bible expresses in Psalm 33:12, "Blessed is the nation whose God is their Lord, the people he chose for his inheritance. Pray that the nation would turn from wickedness and back to the commands of God.

- Pray for those who are sick. Pray for their healing.

- Pray for an economic incline. Many are suffering from poverty and lack.

1. Pray for restoration of marriages.

2. Pray for those who are fighting the war in Iraq. Pray that God would protect their lives.

3. Pray against murders, suicide, and crimes of all kinds.

When to pray?

"Pray without ceasing." (1 Thessalonians 5:17) This

doesn't mean that you have go throughout the entire day on your knees or being emotional in your verbiage. This command of scripture simply expresses that one should include God in their daily thoughts throughout the day. These prayers don't have to be exhaustive or filled with repetitive eloquent words. It's simply honoring and recognizing God throughout your day. For example, expressing a simple "Thank you Lord" throughout the day will suffice as prayer without ceasing. Now, you should also understand that as you grow in prayer, you will develop a set time of prayer. Some may have their alone prayer time in the mornings when they awaken, for others in the evenings when they arrive home from work, and for the "owls" who are awake during the midnight hour, their personal prayer time with God is during the wee hours of the night. Know which time of prayer works best for you and God.

Where to pray?

Truthfully, there is no set physical location where one should pray. However, where you pray is important when you are seeking God in prayer. You want to pray in a location and area that is free of distractions. If you are praying at home, find a quiet place. Some of you may have a prayer room that is ideal for your prayer time with God. If you are praying at work, make sure your prayer doesn't disturb your co workers. If you pray radically, you may want to pray at home. Of course you can pray at church. You can pray in your car, in the shower, in your home office, or at a prayer meeting. These are just a few of many places where you can pray.

Why pray?

Prayer is the breathing force to one's spirit. Because prayer is dialogue with God, when you do not pray, your spirit does not have the "oxygen" it needs to sustain spiritually. Prayer brings life to the spirit of a man. There are a plethora of reasons one should pray, inclusive of the following:

1. Prayer brings one closer to God. There is a need for connectivity at the very core of our being. Prayer is connecting to God. When you pray, it deepens your connection with God.

2. Prayer is a command given by God. The Bible expresses in Philippians 4:6-7, "Be anxious for nothing, but in everything by PRAYER and supplication with thanksgiving, let your request be made known to God."

3. Prayer gives us solutions. When we have inquiries, queries, and problems, prayer will serve as the solution. God will give us an answer in prayer.

4. Prayer demonstrates that we have faith. Without faith it is impossible to please God. When we pray, we are demonstrating to God that we have faith in him.

5. Prayer alleviates our sorrows and weariness (Matthew

11:28). When we experience pain of all kinds, we can find solace and comfort in prayer. We serve a God who is not deaf to our prayers.

6. Prayer assists with overcoming the temptations of life. When you place your focus on scriptures and Jesus, it weakens the temptation you're presented with.

7. Prayer is a weapon of spiritual warfare. You have an arch nemesis, Satan who sends darts in the spirit to buffet you. When you pray, you release arsenal in the spirit realm against Satan and his kingdom

How to pray?

Praying is synonymous to riding a bike, you must learn how. As you learn, you become better at it. In order to pray effectively, you have to allow the Holy Spirit to lead and guide you into prayer. The foundation of prayer is the word of God. The more time that you spend reading and ingesting the word of God, the more intense and effective your prayer life will be. You will begin to grow in prayer as you spend time in the word of God. There is no set rubric on how to pray, as each child of God prays differently. However, in the Bible, the disciples asked Jesus to teach them how to pray (Luke 11:1). Jesus replied to his disciples, "When you pray, say: Our Father, which art in Heaven, hallowed be thy name. Thy kingdom come. Thy will be done, as in heaven, so in earth. Give us this day our daily bread. And forgive us our sins; for we also forgive everyone that is indebted to us. And lead us not into temptation; but deliver us from evil (Luke 11:2-4, KJV)."

If you are a beginner at prayer, this model prayer can be a starting point for you. Recite this prayer until your prayer life increases. Again, as you spend more time with God, your prayer language will increase and become more intimate.

CHAPTER 2: POWER OF PRAYER

What comes to mind when you think about the word power? Some words that come to mind when I think of power include: dominance, authority, strength, mastery, and acceleration. According to the Miriam Webster dictionary, power is defined as the ability or capability of doing or accomplishing something. As a believer, God has given you power through the medium of prayer. The power of prayer resides in God. In 1 John 5:14-15, the Bible expresses, "This is the confidence we have in approaching God: that if we ask anything according to his will, he hears us. And if we know he hears us, whatever we ask, we know that we have what we asked of him."

Have you ever prayed and it seemed like God was ignoring your prayer? Maybe you prayed earnestly for something and it never happened. Maybe you prayed to God about a situation and he didn't give you the answer that you so desperately wanted. I can only imagine the disappointment and perplexing emotional duress that you may have felt subsequent to your "perceived" unanswered prayer. The Bible expresses that the effectual fervent prayers availeth much. The word avail is the Greek word for "ischuo." Ischuo means to give strength and wholeness. One can infer that prayer gives strength and wholeness to the one making petitions before the Lord. Let's take a look at a few of our biblical predecessors who exercised the power of prayer and then we will discuss the power of prayer in our own lives.

Elijah

Elijah was known as one of the greatest prophets in the Old Testament. Elijah was a man like you and I, but when he prayed the Heavens responded. Elijah knew how to pray effectively. He knew how to get answers from his prayers. Elijah prayed earnestly that it would not rain, and it did not rain on the land for three and a half years. Again he prayed, and the heavens gave rain and the earth produced its crops (James 5:17, 18). Listen! That's some pretty effective prayers. When one can pray about atmospheric precipitation and heaven responds to their prayer, that is pretty powerful. Upon deeper examination of Elijah's life and prayer, one can conclude the following:

A. Elijah was a prophet who possessed faith. Faith is a key element to exhibiting the power of prayer and getting God to respond. He believed in God and he didn't doubt that God would come through for him.

B. Because Elijah possessed faith, he was able to hear God. Earlier, I explained that prayer is dialogue with God. Faith comes by hearing the word of God. Because of his prophetic vocation, he was able to hear God audibly. Elijah prayed in FAITH. Without faith, it is impossible to please God. With faith, coupled with prayer, Elijah pleased God and was able to get God to respond to his prayer.

C. Elijah prayed humbly and persistently. Elijah practiced humility and his prayers were persistent.

D. Elijah prayed with a definitive goal in mind. He knew what he wanted and he was intentional about his prayer. He was focused and not distracted by outside hindrances.

Paul and Silas

The biblical account of Paul and Silas' prison experience can be found in Acts chapter 16. Here's a synopsis of the text. Paul and Silas went to Philippi to teach the gospel. There was a girl who was controlled by an evil spirit that followed Paul and Silas. She would cry out "these are the servants of the Most High God." Although her words were true, the intent of her words were that of mockery. Paul then cast out the evil spirit that had once ruled the girl. The girl's master was upset with Paul because this girl was a fortune teller. Her masters were accustomed to making money from the demonically controlled gift of fortune telling. Since the girl was no longer vexed with the spirit, she was unprofitable to her master. Subsequent to this, her master had Paul and Silas thrown into prison, proclaiming that they were causing confusion.

The Bible records that Paul and Silas were beaten severely. However, at midnight, Paul and Silas prayed and sang hymns of praise to God. An earthquake then shook the prison. Everyone's shackles were removed from their arms and legs. That is the power of prayer.

Hezekiah

The bible records the prayer of Hezekiah and his health dilemma in the book of Isaiah in chapter 38. Hezekiah was sick unto death. The prophet Isaiah warned Hezekiah that he was soon to die and that he should get his house in order. Hezekiah, with tears in his eyes, turned his face to the wall, and he prayed the following prayer: "Remember, Lord, how I have walked before you faithfully and with wholehearted devotion and have done what is good in your eyes." God heard Hezekiah's prayer and responded by telling the prophet Isaiah to go back to Hezekiah and to tell him that the Lord has heard his prayer and has seen his tears. As a result of Hezekiah's prayer, God extended 15 years to his life. That is the power of prayer.

There are various other biblical accounts on the power of prayer. Prayer has conquered death (2 Kings 4:3-6), removed depression (Psalm 42), and defeated enemies (Psalm 6). Know that God is NOT a genie and there is no magic formula as it pertains to prayer. When you pray to God from a pure heart and a contrite spirit, coupled with praying according to his will, he will respond to your prayers. Many of our prayers don't get answered the way that we would like, because we ask amiss or according to our human desires. Praying for a husband that God didn't approve of won't get God's approval. Praying for a million dollars to be seen by man, probably won't get God's approval. To experience the full manifestation of power in prayer, examine your heart, be self reflexive of your motives, and pray for God's will to be done in your life. The same way that God answered the prayers of the aforementioned biblical predecessors, he can answer your prayers. As we have examined the prayers of Elijah, Paul and Silas, and Hezekiah, we can conclude that there is power in prayer. God moved supernaturally with rain for Elijah. God responded to the prayers of Paul and Silas and allowed an earthquake to shake the place that held them in bondage. God rebuked death subsequent to Hezekiah's prayers. In prayer, God can move on your behalf. He can heal your sick body, restore your broken marriage, remove the stain on past heartbreak, and restore your relationship with your family members. Think about the times that you prayed for your personal healing. Recall the prayers that God answered for your previously. Think about your relatives that received salvation subsequent to your prayers. You exercised the power of prayer. There are many occasions where the power of prayer was evident in my life. I have prayed for people who received supernatural healing, some instantaneously, and others over time. I have prayed for favor in areas and God answered my petitions. I admonish you today to use the power of prayer!

CHAPTER 3: TYPES OF PRAYER

There are variations of types of prayer found in the Bible. There is a modicum of variations of prayer mentioned implicitly and explicitly throughout the bible. This chapter will examine a few of the types of prayer. I admonish you to continue to study and expand your research on the many other types of prayer as you grow in prayer.

Prayer of Intercession

This is the type of prayer where you pray on the behalf of others. Intercession entails intervening between two people, to speak on the behalf of someone else to another person. In this type of prayer, you pray to God on behalf of someone else.

Prayer of Faith

Without faith, it is impossible to please God. Faith is the substance of things hoped for and the evidence of things not seen. Faith is believing, even if there is no tangible evidence of there being a possible manifestation of what's being believed in faith. The bible records in the book of James chapter 5, that the prayer of faith will heal the sick. This type or prayer is offered with complete assurance that God will answer the prayer, despite what it looks like.

Warfare Prayer

This type of prayer involves using prayer as a weapon against the adversary, Satan. The bible expresses in Ephesians 6:10-13, "Finally, my brethren, be strong in the Lord, and in the power of his might. Put on the whole armor of God, that ye may be able to stand against the wiles of the devil. For we wrestle not against flesh and blood, but against principalities, against powers, against the rulers of the darkness of this world, against spiritual wickedness in high places. Wherefore take unto you the whole armor of God, that you may be able to withstand in the evil day, and having done all to stand, stand." Spiritual warfare exists in the unseen, spiritual dimension, where God is all-powerful and Satan is in rebellion.

The moment you became a Christian, is the moment you were enlisted in God's army. Prayer is arsenal against Satan. Spiritual warfare is the resistance, overcoming, and conquering of Satan's attacks, temptations, deceptions, and lies. The battlefield in spiritual warfare is the mind. Satan fights God's soldiers in their minds. There are 3 areas that Satan specifically fights God's soldiers, inclusive of the following: temptation, deception, and accusations. When you pray, you avert Satan's weapons against you and then he is hit with spiritual darts through the weapon of prayer.

Corporate Prayer

This is a time of gathering together to pray in a communal setting. Prayers are prayed in a group atmosphere and offered unto God. The bible expresses in Matthew 18:20, "For where two or three are gathered together in my name, there I am in their midst." Corporate prayer also entails being in spiritual agreement. There is power in corporate prayer (Matthew 18:19).

Private Prayer

This type of prayer is individualistic, intimate, and personal. This prayer is not seen by anyone but God, as the individual prays to God in private. In the book of Matthew chapter 6, the Lord tells the disciples to pray in private. He didn't want the disciples to pray as a means to be seen by men. Christ didn't want the disciples to pray Pharisaical prayers. Christ expressed to the disciples that hypocrites pray loud so that they can be seen by men. It is in private prayer where God sees the heart of the individual.

Prayer of Praise and Thanksgiving

This type of prayer expresses adoration, gratitude, praise, and thanksgiving unto God. There is so much to be thankful for. This time in prayer entails verbal expression to God that you are grateful and thankful unto Him. Some scriptural references of prayers of praise and thanksgiving include: Psalm 100, Psalm 107, and 1 Chronicles 29.

Prayer of Supplication

The Hebrew word for supplication means "a request or

petition. Supplication simply means to ask God for something. In other words, the prayer of supplication is making a request unto God. In the New Testament or Covenant, Matthew 6:11 clearly gives us a depiction of the prayer of supplication by asking to given our daily bread.

Imprecatory or Prayer of Judgment

To imprecate means to judge or to speak evil against someone. This prayer was associated with the prayer of king David. This is not a prayer of revenge, but a prayer that is in divine agreement with God's judgment. These prayers are not prayers of hate and vengeance. Some examples of David's imprecatory prayers can be found in Psalms 7, 35, 58, and 59.

Consecration Prayer

To consecrate is to set apart or dedicate to God for a higher purpose. When you pray a consecration prayer, you should be on a fast and abstaining from all forms of distraction while communing with God in prayer. This type of prayer requires sacrifice on your part. Your flesh is decreased, but spiritually you are able to receive from God clearly because of your willingness to sacrifice in consecration.

Prayer of Worship

This is an intimate prayer with God. The primary focus of this prayer is pleasing God. This prayer focuses on who God is. In the book of Matthew (chapter 6), Jesus' model prayer is an example of a prayer of worship.

Prayer of Forgiveness

This type of prayer involves asking God for the forgiveness of sins committed by omission or by commission. This prayer also includes self examination and forgiveness of those who have wronged you or have offended you.

CHAPTER 4: BIBLICAL WOMEN & PRAYER

There are various accounts of women who prayed in the bible. However, this chapter will focus on the prayers of a few biblical women and will dissect their lives and prayers. Ride with me on this journey, because you may find yourself living vicariously through these biblical women.

Esther

Who was Esther? Esther was a Jewish, orphan girl who was adopted by her uncle Mordecai after the death of her parents. After Queen Vashti was dethroned, the position of queen was open and all of the young women in the province who were young, beautiful virgins, were brought before the king after 1 year of preparation. Even in a room full of 10's, ghetto terminology- dime pieces, Esther was able to win. God had granted Esther favor and she was crowned queen of Persia. God used Esther's beauty and grace to capture the king's heart. Esther followed her uncle's instructions by fasting and praying for her people and saved her people from being annihilated. Many of you reading this book are like Esther. Your past may have been filled with pain. Yet, God is placing his favor upon you and you're about to be crowned with splendor and favor. God will set you above your expectations. I can surmise that Esther had a powerful prayer life based on the outcome of her people being vindicated.   The bible expresses in Esther 4:16 (KJV) "Go, gather together all the Jews that are present in Shushan, and fast ye for me, and neither eat nor drink three days, night or day: I also and my maidens will fast likewise; and so will I go in unto the king, which *is* not according to the law: and if I perish, I perish." In this text, pray is implied. They fasted for 3 days and for 3 nights. Fasting by itself, would have just been refraining from food. However, in the Old Testament, fasting was accompanied by prayer. This means that they fasted and prayed before Esther went before the king with her concern. As a result of her prayer and fast, her people were saved from being annihilated. Don't you know that your prayers can save your family and future generation? You've been equipped with the same anointing as Esther.

Hannah

Hannah was the wife of Elkanah. She was also barren and unable to have children. She was one of the two wives of Elkanah. Penninah, Elkanah's other wife, bore children to Elkanah. In modern terms, Hannah would be considered as the "main chick. Although she was the main wife, she was unable to conceive. Hannah's prayer life was on "fleek" and consistent. She prayed earnestly for a child. Even through her disappointment of not being able to bare children, she prayed. Hannah was desperate. On one occasion (1 Samuel 1:10), Hannah prayed and asked God for a son. She vowed to give this son back to God. Eli the priest blessed Hannah and she returned home. Hannah then conceived and gave birth to Samuel. She then conceived 3 sons and 2 daughters. Maybe you have been unable to conceive children. Maybe the doctors have pronounced bareness to your womb. You can stand on faith and pray through as Hannah prayed. Maybe you find it hard to give birth to the vision, business, book, relationship, or friendship that you so desire.

Use prayer as the catalyst to birthing out the very thing that you have petitioned God for in prayer.

The Woman at the Well

The bible mentions in John 4:5-42, a woman at the well who was thirsty for truth. She had "prayer" or a conversation with Jesus. During this one on one dialogue, Jesus was exhausted from a long day's journey and he made a stop at Jacob's well. This woman was at the well with a jar in her hand. Jesus asked the woman if she would give him a drink of water (John 4:7). She replied by focusing on their differences in background as she was a Samaritan and Jesus was a Jew. Jews were not supposed to speak to Samaritans. Jesus said to her "If you knew the gift of God, and who it is that saith to thee, give me to drink; thou wouldest have asked of him, and he would have given thee living water. The conversation between the woman at the well and Jesus continued. Jesus went on to say "Whoever drinks the water that I give him will never thirst (John 4:14)." Jesus then told her to call her husband to come back. She confessed and replied that she did not have a husband. He then told her that she had five husbands and the man that she had now is not her husband. In John 4:26, Jesus reveals his identity to her. She left the well with joy and told others "Come see a man who told me everything I ever did." Maybe you are like the woman at the well. Maybe you have a sordid past. Maybe you've slept with a lot of men and were a whore. However, one encounter with Jesus can change your entire life. When you drink of the living water, he can cleanse you from the past sins that you may have committed. Your past has passed and you have encountered the well that never runs dry.

Deborah

Deborah was a judge and prophetess who feared and reverenced God. On one occasion, she told the army general Barak, that God had spoken to her and that God had promised victory to Barak. Deborah's word to Barak came to pass and Barak's army defeated the army of Sisera. Deborah responded with a prayer of thanksgiving and praise unto God (Judges 5). Maybe God has called you to dominate in the judicial and government matters. Allow him to speak to and through you and execute his instructions. As a result, you will see victory in your life and in the lives of those connected to you. Without wavering or doubting God, you must execute his word. Then, you will be able to praise and thank God that he has fulfilled his word.

Lydia

Lydia was a biblical "boss chick." She was a business woman during biblical times. She was also extremely wealthy. Lydia had a powerful prayer life. She had gathered together women to pray and to hear the gospel. She had a commitment to prayer. She knew that pray was not self centered and she understood the importance of women supporting one another in prayer. Maybe you are like Lydia. You love God and you have been called to the marketplace. You are about your business. You understand investments, entrepreneurial lingo, the importance of team work, and residual income. Yet, you also understand that prayer is vital to the flourishing of your business endeavors. You may also have this innate drive to support other women in prayer. You're just like Lydia- a boss and a prayer warrior.

Anna

Anna was a widow who was known to be a consistent prayer warrior. She would pray in the temple constantly. She prayed whenever and wherever. She did not allow her loss of her husband restrict her from communing with God. You may be a widow. You may feel like the loss of your spouse has numbed you from praying to God. However, you have to allow time and God to heal you from those wounds.

CHAPTER 5: BIBLICAL PRAYERS

Hey pretty girls! This chapter gives biblical depictions of the prayers that our biblical predecessors prayed. The corresponding scriptures are included for your personal study and review.

The Lord's Prayer (Matthew 6:9-13)

"After this manner therefore pray ye: Our Father which art in heaven, Hallowed be thy name. Thy kingdom come, thy will be done in earth, as it is in heaven. Give us this day our daily bread. And forgive us our debts, as we forgive our debtors. And lead us not into temptation but deliver us from evil: For thine is the kingdom, and the power, and the glory, forever. Amen."

Jesus prayed this prayer as a model guide. It is a patterned prayer that expresses that "what" and "how" components of prayer.

Prayer of Jabez (1 Chronicles 4:10)

This was a prayer that Jabez prayed in reference to protection and finances.

"And Jabez called on the God of Israel, saying, Oh that thou wouldest bless me indeed, and enlarge my coast, and that thine hand might be with me, and that thou wouldest keep me from evil, that it may not grieve me."

Solomon's Prayer (1 Kings 3:6-9)

Solomon prayed to God for wisdom in the following prayer.

"You have shown us great and steadfast love to your servant David my father, because he walked before you in faithfulness, in righteousness, and in uprightness of heart toward you. And you have kept for him this great and steadfast love and have given him a son to sit on his throne this day. And now, O Lord my God, you have made your servant king in place of David my father, although I am but a little child. I do not know how to go out or come in. And your servant is in the midst of your people who you have chosen, a great people, too many to be numbered or counted for multitude. Give your servant therefore an understanding mind to govern your people, that I may discern between good and evil, for who is able to govern this your great people?"

Ok girls! After reading about the prayers of our biblical predecessors, you should have a greater understanding of the various types of prayers that they prayed. This can also serve as a guide to your own personal prayers. Have you ever asked God to restore your heart? To revive your spirit? To forgive your sins? To bless your finances? I know that I have. As I have reviewed the prayers of the aforementioned, it serves as a blueprint on how to effectively pray through.

CHAPTER 6: PRAYER WATCHES

Hey girls! Have you ever walked passed the jewelry counter at a jewelry store and noticed the various types of luxury watches? How did it make your feel? Hopefully, not broke lol. There's an overwhelming sense of exhilaration and excitement that I feel when I look at the array of watches on display at the jewelry store. I have an admiration for beautiful diamond watches. I think a woman with a beautiful watch on her wrist, is a woman who understands class and grace. Having a beautiful watch on your wrist expresses that your time is valuable and you don't have time to waste. I like various watches including watches made by Gucci, Cartier, Michael Kors, and Rolex. The precious metals that are used to make these watches, require great detail and tedious hours of work by watch makers. From a natural or secular perspective, the sole purpose of a watch is to keep up with time. From a spiritual perspective, watch is insight into the spiritual realm. The Bible expresses in 1 Kings 9:17-18 that we are to be watchmen and to warn those who are in danger. When we pray, we watch over ourselves, our homes, our relatives, our friends, our cities, our regions, and our nation.

Prayer, metaphorically speaking, can be considered as eyes in the spirit. When you pray, you watch, and are given insight, and at times foresight in the spirit realm. When you "watch" in the spirit, you are looking for the enemy's tactics as well as Gods directives. If we watch out for the enemy's tactics, we can avert his arsenal weapons. Our nemesis is Satan and his plan is to steal, kill, and destroy. If we are watchman in prayer, we can counterattack his weapons through the "watch" and weapon of prayer.

There are 24 hours in a given day. The Bible makes reference to "watches, which are periods of time during the day or night. As your prayer life increases, you will be led by the Holy Spirit to pray during a specified watch. Every Christian believer has been assigned a prayer watch. Some may be unaware of the aforementioned, because they haven't spent time with God in prayer. Have you ever been awakened during the wee hours of the night such as 3 a.m. on various occasions? That was probably God trying to wake you up to pray. The Bible expresses in Habakkuk 2:1 (clause A), "I will stand upon my watch, and set me upon the tower, and will watch to see what he will say unto me. Pretty girl, you've been assigned a prayer watch by God. Ask God to reveal to you which prayer watch you've been assigned to.

The 8 Prayer Watches:

Again, there are 24 hours in a day. There are 8 prayer watches that are divided into 3 hour increments. I will briefly give a synopsis of each of the prayer watches.

First Prayer Watch 6 p.m. to 9 p.m.

This prayer watch is two fold and includes: a time of quiet reflection and a period of covenant renewal with God. During your time of prayer, be still and quiet your spirit. This is the time to settle your mind. After you have come home from work or from your business, meditate on the word of God. Realign your mind with the word of God. Ask God for directives and strategies for the future. If you have an Apostolic calling on your life, this may be the prayer watch that you have been called to. Also, this watch is a time to ask God to release his covenant blessings that he has promised to you and his people.

Second Prayer Watch 9 p.m. to 12 a.m.

This prayer watch is the time for divine judgment. This is the time that intercessors are able to significantly impact the spiritual realm before the enemy starts his attacks. During this prayer watch, revelation flows heavily from the throne of Heaven. This is also the time for tearing down spiritual walls of darkness.

Third Prayer Watch 12 a.m. to 3 a.m.

This prayer watch is the breaking day watch. This is the period of time where the most demonic activity occurs in the realm of the spirit. Its also known as the darkest hour. Satan operates heavily in this hour because most people are asleep during this time. This prayer watch is for those who are seasoned and equipped in prayer. Those who have been called to this prayer watch understand how to use prayer as their spiritual armor against Satan. During this time, watchman is to pray against demonic activity, against satanic attacks, and for Gods protection to overtake the lives of their families, churches, state, and nation. This is a time of spiritual warfare (Ephesians 6). As a watchman during this hour, you must fight in prayer against every plot, incantation, spell, and hex that has been assigned to the lives of Gods people by the adversary.

Fourth Prayer Watch 3 a.m. to 6 a.m.

This is the time to command your morning. This prayer watch is vital because it is the last prayer watch of the night. The satanic hosts that were sent out by Satan are now returning to their base. During this time, you should command your morning by speaking into the atmosphere what you expect for your day. Speak against demonic attacks and hindrances that would try to buffet you. Command your day to be filled with Gods peace, strength, and love. This is also the time for you to declare Gods word.

Fifth Prayer Watch 6 a.m. to 9 a.m.

This is the time that God gives strength to his watchman. This is also the time when God prepares the watchman for service.   In the natural, this is the time during the beginning of sunrise. In the spirit, this is the time for an outpouring of Gods spirit, healing, and peace. As the sun rises in the earth, the Son rises over the people of God during this prayer watch.

Sixth Prayer Watch 9 a.m. to 12 p.m.

This is the time where the watchman will see God manifest his divine promises. This is also the time to reflect on Gods saving and keeping power. This was the hour when the children of Israel's prayers were answered. Subsequent to their prayer, they received an answer from God concerning their journey to the promise land. This prayer watch is the time that watchman should be in expectancy for their harvest.

Seventh Payer Watch 12 p.m. to 3 p.m.

This is the time for the watchman to seek the Lord. This is also the time of rest. 3 p.m. during biblical times was known as the hour of prayer. This prayer watch occurs during mid day. This is the time to seek God and to rest in God. The Bible expresses in Psalm 91:1, "He that dwelleth in the secret place of the Most High God shall abide under the shadow of the Almighty. The watchman should make God their habitation during this time of prayer.

Eighth Prayer Watch 3 p.m. to 6 p.m.

This prayer watch carries much significance because it was during this time that Jesus Christ was crucified and died on the cross. He died so that you and I could have eternal life. Because of his shed blood, we can come boldly before the throne of grace in prayer. This is time where the watchman is to take on the cross of Christ and die to self, while living in Christ. This is also the time that the watchman should rejoice in the power of Jesus' resurrection from the grave. This is also the time to seek God for his wisdom, revelation, and truth.

Specified Prayers

During each of the 8 prayer watches, watchman should pray specified prayers on the following areas of concentration. I have provided some examples of areas of prayer in congruence with the respective prayer watch. In the following table, I have listed the prayer watch and what to pray for during that time of prayer. You may use this as a guide when praying during your specified hour of prayer.

Prayer Watch	What to Pray For
First	Pray strategically that God would remove curses. Pray for the renewal of covenant. Pray for God's guidance.
Second	Pray for God's protection, guidance, and for the kingdom of darkness to be defeated.
Third	Pray against demonic forces and their attacks. Pray against famine, plane crashes, divorce, and illnesses. Pray for God's peace to overtake his people.
Fourth	Pray against the plans of the enemy. Pray for God to cover your day. Pray for the will of God to be manifested in the lives of God's people.
Fifth	Pray that the Holy Spirit would prepare you for the day. Plead the blood of Jesus over yourself, your friends, and relatives. Pray for God's redemption.
Sixth	Pray for strength, forgiveness, prosperity, joy, holiness, and endurance.
Seventh	Pray against all satanic darts. Pray for an upright walk with Christ. Pray that your light would illuminate in the earth realm. Pray for the salvation of the unsaved.
Eighth	Pray for complete surrenderence to Christ. Pray for wholeness, peace, and righteousness.

CHAPTER 7: MODEL PRAYERS

I will be the first to admit that I wasn't always equipped in prayer. Like many of you reading this book, I was a novice and barely knew one scripture when I rededicated my life back to Christ over 15 years ago. I think the only scripture that I knew by heart was John 3:16. I believe I knew that scripture because it was engrained in my memory from Sunday school when I was a child. When I was a babe in Christ, I was so hungry for the word of God. I would go to church 4 to 5 times a week. I was hungry for knowledge and I just wanted more of God. There were some days that I would go to the library for hours to read the word of God. I was intense and intentional about getting closer to God. I paid close attention to how the scriptures expressed how Jesus prayed. As my knowledge of the word of God increased, so did my prayer life. The Holy Spirit gave me utterance and I soon had a heavenly language that I also learned to pray in. As I grew in my walk with Christ, my prayers expanded. I began to pray the word of God. In the coming pages of this chapter, I have included model prayers that the Lord has given me.

Use these prayers as model prayers. I pray that these prayers will assist you in your spiritual growth. Whether you are a novice in prayer or a seasoned intercessor, there's always room for growth in the area of prayer. Pretty girls let's pray!

FINANCES

Father, teach me how to properly obtain, acquire, and replicate money. Father, give me the resources and currency to survive economically. Give me the financial strategies to live a debt free life. Teach me how to correct all past financial mistakes that I have made. Establish your covenant of prosperity with me. Heaven and Earth bear record, I am in agreement that the economic downfall in the U.S. doesn't belong to me. Eradicate the paycheck to paycheck mentality and cycle. Break the spirits of poverty and lack. Lord, you are my source. Make provisions for me. I pray the prayer of Jabez, "Oh that thou wouldest bless me indeed, and enlarge my coast, and that thine hand might be with me, and that thou wouldest keep me from evil, that it may not grieve thee (1 Chronicles 4:10). I decree and declare that I am blessed coming in and blessed going out. My barns and vats will overflow with new wine and with new oil. I decree in the atmosphere that I am the lender and not the borrower. My name will be associated with wealth. I prophesy to my bank account that it will grow exponentially and that I will never be broke another day in my life. The word of God declares in Deuteronomy 8:18, that we should remember the Lord our God, for it is he that gives us the power to obtain wealth.

RELATIONSHIPS

I pray for mutually exclusive healthy relationships to be in my life. May there be synergy, trust, and respect in covenant ordained relationships. Every demonic relationship shall be severed. Expose those who operate from a Jezebel, Delilah, Leviathan, and/or Judas spirit. Remove every person that is not conducive to my destiny. Cultivate every God ordained covenant connection. May covenant relationships that were severed prematurely be restored. Father, I pray that you would remove every toxic relationship. Give me that ability to discern the motives of those who enter into my life.

REJECTION

I pray that I would be free from the spirit of rejection. Every defense mechanism that I created as a result of past rejection is now removed. Lord, I submit to your overwhelming love and peace. Rejection causes anger, bitterness, fear, and hatred. Rejection has not allowed me to accept me. Today, I make peace with myself. I make peace with God. I decree an increase in my self esteem. I was created to be loved and accepted. The word of God declares that "when my father and mother forsake me, then the Lord will take me up." (Psalms 27:10) I am accepted into the beloved. Amen.

THE MIND

Housed within the mind is the will of man, emotional responses, voluntary and involuntary movements, thoughts, and intellect. The mind is the central processing unit of the body. The mind is the battleground where the enemy sends attacks. Lord, keep and guard my mind from Satan's devices. Isaiah 26:6 declares, "thou wilt keep him (her) in perfect peace, whose mind is stayed on thee because he (she) trusteth in thee. It is my prayer that I would possess the peace of God. Father, break aberrant thoughts, false ideologies, emotional scars from past traumas, father issues, mother issues, deep rejections, abandonment, low self-esteem, unhealthy recidivism in relationships, and vein imaginations. Lord I pray that you would remove emotional struggles raging within. Cleanse my mind from perversions. Confusion has to flee my mind. I pull down the stronghold of confusion. I fire back every arrow of mind destruction fired against my mind in the name of Jesus. I pull down every stronghold of uncontrollable thoughts and bring into captivity every area of my thought life to the obedience of Christ. Lord, I pray that you would purge my mind from pride, fear, anxiety, confusion, arrogance, vanity, narcissism, bitterness, forgiveness, jealousy, envy, deception, condemnation, incoherence, and ignorance. Lord, I ask that you would eradicate depression, suicidal ideations, bipolar disorder, schizophrenia, body dysmorphic disorder, sleep terrors, insomnia, fear, phobias, mania, hallucinations, and all forms of psychological bondages. May the peace of God that transcends all understanding, guard my heart and my mind in Christ Jesus. Lord, I petition you today, asking that you would remove all of the baggage from my past. Remove past verbal abuse, word scars, past psychological traumas, and insecurities. Father, free me from daddy issues, unhealthy relational addictions, and toxic thinking. I declare freedom in my mind. I possess the mind of Christ and I am thinking on things that are good, lovely, and of a good report. Amen.

FORGIVENESS

Father, I know that I have sinned against you. I repent of my words and deeds that were sinful. I am truly sorry, and now I want to turn away from my past sinful life. Lord, please forgive me. I pray that you would forgive me of the times that I have been idle with time. Forgive me for idolatry and for placing things and people before you. I ask that you would forgive me for being desensitized to the needs of my fellow brothers and sisters. I repent for being idle, lazy, in doubt of your word, and for consulting with others before coming to you. Lord, I ask that you would remove all unforgiveness from my heart. I release all offenses. As you have forgiven me of my trespasses, I forgive those who have wronged me. Amen.

MARRIAGE

Father, you are a God who honors covenant. I pray that you would touch and breathe upon my marital covenant. I pray that the love in my marriage would be free flowing and unconditional. I pray that my spouse and I would honor, respect, and cherish one another. I pray that my spouse and I would have an understanding of each other's love language. I decree that adultery will not be permitted in my marriage. I decree in the atmosphere that my spouse and I will honor our marital vows. I pray that my spouse and I would be considerate of each other's needs, concerns, and time. I pray that we would be selfless and would be supportive towards one another. Help us to be understanding and forgiving of human weaknesses and frailties. I pray Lord, that you would bless our marriage and that the fruit of love would flourish in our marriage.

DIVORCE

Father, I pray that you would restore me. Divorce has taken a toll on me. It almost feels like a death occurred. Lord, I pray that you would comfort my heart. The grief, shock, anger, resentment, denial, and depression that have come into my life, as a result of the divorce, has to leave me NOW. I speak peace to my mind and spirit. I bind the spirit of rejection and I loose the spirit of adoption of the Father to be upon me now. I have been accepted into the beloved. I release myself from shame and guilt that is associated with the divorce. I decree that I shall live a full life even after divorce. Father, keep me in the arms of your bosom during this trying time of divorce. Amen.

SPIRITUAL WARFARE

May the 4 spirits of Heaven and the 4 chariots fight against every demonic force. Father, I pray that you would blow your ruach breath from the 4 winds of Heaven. Let there be spiritual victory in my life. I take authority over the works of Satan. I bind Satan, every principality, dark power, ruler of darkness, and spiritual wickedness in high places. I loose angelic hosts in the realm of the spirit to war against every demonic trap, wile, and entrapment. I uproot all plans of the adversary and curse them at the root in the name of Jesus. Every Satanic trap is canceled, nullified, and rendered of no effect in the name of Jesus. According to Isaiah 54:17, "No weapon formed against me shall prosper. I decree destruction upon Satan's traps and weapons. When the enemy comes in like a flood, the spirit of the Lord will lift up a standard against him. I understand that according to Ephesians 6, the weapons of my warfare are not carnal. I do not fight against flesh and blood. I am fighting a spiritual battle. Teach my hands to war Father. I will use the spiritual weapons of prayer, praise, and worship to avert the enemy's plots and ploys.

SOUL TIES

I renounce all demonic covenants, vows, pacts, promises, curses to which I have been exposed or made liable by my own actions or by the actions of others. By the act and decision of my own free will, Father, in the name of Jesus. Lord, I ask that you would cleanse my spirit and soul from all soul ties. Let not the enemy persecute my soul. I renounce every vow and commitment that I made with ungodly associations and connections. Lord, I ask for forgiveness for my sins. Lord, I bind the spirits of Incubus and Succubus that have attached to my spirit as a result of soul ties. Lord, I pray that you would deliver my soul from all evil. Lord, I ask that you would root out, remove, and loose me from every soul tie. In Jesus' name, Amen.

DIRECTION

The steps of a good man are ordered by the Lord. Father, you know the way that I should take. Lead and guide me into all truth. Direct my path. I will be like a tree planted by the rivers of water. I will stand still until the appointed time. I will not waver to the left or to the right, but I will follow the leading and guidance of the Holy Spirit. Father, you are my compass. Give me direction concerning my destiny. Bring my life into divine alignment with your will. Have your way in my life. Lead me to the rock that is higher than I. Father, I pray for direction today. You are the way, the truth, and the life. Your word is a lamp unto my feet and a light unto my path. When I can't seem to find my way, I pray that you would guide me. You are my my map and compass. Show me the way in which I should take. I know that you will lead and guide me into all truth. Thank you for ordering my steps. Amen.

SALVATION

Father, I acknowledge to you that I am a sinner. I am remorseful for my sin. I need and ask for forgiveness. I believe that your only begotten Son Jesus Christ shed His precious blood on the cross at Calvary and died for my sins, and I am now willing to turn from my sin. You said in your Word, in Romans 10:9, "that if we confess the Lord our God and believe in our hearts that God raised Jesus from the dead, we shall be saved." I make the confession that Jesus is the savior of my soul. With my heart, I believe that God raised Jesus from the dead. I accept Jesus Christ as my own personal Savior and according to His Word. Thank you Lord for saving me from my sins. Lord Jesus transform my life so that I may bring glory and honor to you. Amen.

PROTECTION

Father, I call on your name today. I decree that the name of the Lord is a strong tower, I run in and find safety. I dwell in the secret place of the Most High God. Lord, I pray that you would dispatch your angels to war on my behalf in the realm of the spirit. Shield me and protect me from all hurt, harm, and danger. Father, I pray that you would protect me from my enemies. The bible declares, "When a man's ways please the Lord, he makes his enemies to be at peace with him."

Father, I pray that you would protect me from those that seek my destruction. I declare that no weapon formed against me shall prosper. Thank you Lord for rescuing me. I thank you for preparing a table before me in the presence of my enemies. Jehovah Gibbor, the mighty Lord in battle, I pray that you would fight for me. Thank you for your divine protection. Amen.

ADDICTIONS

Father, I repent for all sins that I have committed knowingly and unknowingly. I take authority and command all spirits of lying, alcohol, perversion, adultery, idolatry, gluttony, gambling, drugs, and any other addiction to be removed from my life in the name of Jesus. I break all curses that have been spoken over my life. According to Galatians 3:1, "Christ has redeemed from the curse of the law." Lord, I pray for the ability to resist and recognize ploys and temptations of the adversary. I thank you for liberating me from this addiction. I will continue to walk in freedom. Amen.

EMPLOYMENT

Father, your word declares in Ecclesiastes 3:22, "Wherefore I perceive that there is nothing better, than that a man should rejoice in his own works; for that is his portion: for who shall bring him to see what shall be after him?" It is my desire to enjoy the fruit of my labor. I am requesting gainful employment Lord. I turn to you seeking your divine instruction and guidance as I search for employment. I pray that you would grant me your wisdom. Guide my footsteps along the right path, and to lead me to the right employer. Give me the words to say during the interview. It is my desire to use the gifts and talents you have given me in the workplace. Grant this through Christ, our Lord. God be with me today in finding employment. Guide me to a place with an atmosphere of integrity, respect and cooperation. Help me to find fulfillment occupationally and financially. Help me to be confident in knowing your will. Open the right doors for me. please come and direct my path. I believe that in the right timing, I will be hired by an employer according to your will. Amen.

BUSINESS

I pray for financial independence. Lord, I ask that you would give me strategies to effectively run my business. I pray that all fear attached to financial uncertainties would be removed. I pray that the business and marketing plan that I have developed for my business, would attract investors and an array of customers. I pray for an abundance of resources and cash flow. I pray that my business would thrive and would provide the answer to a question in the marketplace. I decree and declare that my product will be needed and utilized all over the world. In Jesus' name, Amen.

STRENGTH

Today, I pray for strength. Lord I need you like never before. I know that your grace is sufficient. For when I am weak, through your power, you are able to make me strong. When I can no longer go on in my human strength, I pray that you would give me supernatural strength. Father, uphold me during times of weakness. I pray that you would strengthen me with all might according to your excellent power. Thank you for granting me with strength. Amen.

GOVERNMENT

Father, your word declares in Jeremiah 29:7 to "seek the welfare of the city where I have sent you into exile, and pray to the Lord on its behalf, for in its welfare you will find your welfare." I pray for my city officials, President, Vice President, House of Representatives, Supreme Court, and every government official that leads this nation. I bring the needs of our government before you and I ask that you would keep and restore our nation. I pray according to 1 Timothy 2:1-3 which expresses, "I exhort therefore, that, first of all, supplications, prayers, intercessions, and giving of thanks, be made for all men; For kings, and for all that are in authority; that we may lead a quiet and peaceable life in all godliness and honesty. For this is good and acceptable in the sight of God our Saviour. "I pray that those in governing authority would receive the wisdom of God, and obey his instructions and wisdom. I pray that this nation would be unified in governing matters. Amen.

HEAVINESS

Father, I ask that you would lift every burden. I pray that the oppression of the enemy would be removed from me. Father, I pray that you would go into my conscious and subconscious and remove any damage placed by past traumatic and abusive experiences. I ask that bad memories be removed from my mind. Any lingering grief that has resided in my mind is being removed in the name of Jesus. Lord, I pray that any memories of pain that have been caused by hurt, trauma, former and present relationships, rejection, and abandonment be eradicated. I loose the garment of praise over my spirit and mind in the name of Jesus. Mourning is being removed and God is giving me the oil of joy. Lord, thank you for lifting the heavy burdens from my life. Amen.

FILLING OF THE HOLY SPIRIT

Father, I know that there is an initial filling, but many refillings. Fill me again. Fill me up, until my cup overflows. Pour out your spirit upon me. Fill me with the knowledge of your will. Restore unto me the joy of thy salvation. I pray that I would be led by the Holy Spirit. I pray that I would walk in the spirit, so that I would not fulfill the desires of the flesh. I pray that I would exhibit the fruit of the spirit. Amen.

WISDOM

Wisdom is the application of knowledge. The beginning of knowledge is the fear of the Lord. Father, I reverence you on this day. I ask that you would grant me the wisdom of Solomon to make sound and just decisions. I decree that when I ask God for wisdom that he would grant it unto me (James 1:5). Father, I pray that you would give me a discerning heart to distinguish between right and wrong. I pray that I would possess the revelation, knowledge, and understanding of God. I will study to show myself approved. I will not be ignorant to the seasons of my life, but will be abreast with the changing of the seasons of my life.

ABUNDANT LIFE

Lord, it is in your that I live, move, and have my being. Thank you for giving me life. You have called me to live the abundant life (John 10:10). I placed on this earth to do more than just pay bills. It is my prayer that I would enjoy all of what life has to offer. I will experience heaven on earth. I will experience joy unspeakable. I will live a life that includes wholeness. I will possess an abundance of joy, peace, prosperity, and thriving relationships. Amen.

FAMILY

Father, I thank you for my family. Protect each of them and shield them in the safety of your arms. Heal those that need to be healed. Give peace where there is calamity. Your word declares that a house divided cannot stand. Allow our familial home to be that of unity. Break every generational curse. May the future generation of this family pass the torch of prosperity, faith, and morale. Cover every member of my family under your blood father. May love flourish amongst every family member. In Jesus' name, I pray, Amen.

LOVE

God is love. As an extension of his DNA, I profess that I am love. Love is the greatest commandment. Father, teach me how to love as you do. Give me wisdom pertaining to the unwavering love that you possess. I decree that I will not dispose of those you have divinely assigned to my life. I also profess that I will love the hell out of my enemies. When disagreements arise in my life, I understand that every disagreement is not grounds for dismissal. I pray that I would possess the heart of God. Remove all offenses and unforgiveness from my heart. Create in me a clean heart and renew a right spirit within me. I want to operate from the love mentioned in 1 Corinthians 13 that expresses that Love is patient, kind, not envious, not boastful, not proud, not rude, not self seeking, not easily angered, and keeps no records of wrongs. It always protects, trusts, hopes, and perseveres. Love never fails. I pray that I would exhibit the love of Christ daily.

HEALING

Father, you are the creator of man. You created the very physicality of man/woman. I pray that you would heal every infirmity that has tried to take residence in my body. Your word declares that healing is the children's bread. I am your child and today I proclaim that healing is MINE. Touch every body system. Every cell that is not life giving is being eradicated from my body in the name of Jesus. Sickness and disease will not be able to reside in my body.

You bore 39 stripes for my healing. HIV, cancers of every kind, reproductive issues, ulcerative colitis, degenerative disc disease, sexually transmitted infections, heart disease, multiple sclerosis, or any other ailment that has illegally entered my body, must be ejected from my temple. I believe that I am healed. I receive my healing in Jesus' name. Amen.

CHAPTER 8: PRETTY GIRL PRAYER

Guess what pretty girl? You have made it to the homestretch of your pretty girls pray journey. This chapter includes the pretty girl prayer, pretty girl affirmations, and a 30-day prayer journal. I'm so excited about your prayer life. Its going to go to a higher trajectory. Whatever you do, don't go a day without talking to God in prayer. Alright! Get ready to pray!

Pretty Girl Prayer

Heavenly Father,

I thank you for creating me and for creating this day. I honor you for who you are. I thank you for leading and guiding my path on this journey called life. I have been fearfully and wonderfully created. I am an extension of God and I possess his DNA, which gives me the ability to reproduce and create. There are treasures locked within my loins. Out of my belly shall flow rivers of living waters. Father, I know that you have given me everything that I need to live the abundant life. I embrace my femininity and the very essence of being a pretty girl. I embrace every aspect of my being including my flaws. You make no mistakes God. I'm here for a purpose and there is a specific assignment that I have been called to do. I will not leave this earth before the appointed time. Lord, I pray for supernatural strength when I am weak in the flesh. I pray that you would strengthen me with all might according to your excellent power. I pray for endurance and the ability to progress forward, despite opposition. Lord, I ask that you open doors that no man can shut. I thank you in advanced for the opportunities that shall come my way. I thank you for my family. I pray that you would touch every person in my family and that you would meet every need. I pray for my ministry leaders, mentors, global leaders, and government officials. I pray for my mind to be receptive to your mind. Grant me peace of mind Father. I speak that my latter days shall be greater than my former. Lord, I know that all things are working together for my good. There is no lack in my life because you have supplied all of my needs. I am seasoning my words with grace, because I know that life and death are in the power of the tongue. Father, I pray that you would utilize me as you see fit. I ask that you would stir up every gift that you have placed within me. My gifts are making room for me and they are bringing me before great men. I will sit amongst the great. Lord, I ask today that you would search my heart and that you would remove anything in my heart that is defiled Create in me a clean heart. I release all unforgiveness of the past. I will not allow offense to remain in my life. I free myself from past pain and trauma. I pray that you would stabilize my emotions. Thank you Lord for everything. May the words of my mouth and the meditation of my heart, be acceptable in your sight Amen.

Affirmations

Affirmations are statements aimed to affect the conscious and subconscious mind.

The words included in these affirmations should inspire, motivate, and empower the person reciting the affirmations. Some benefits of reciting affirmations include: 1)

They negate negative thinking by replacing it with positive words, 2) they influence the mind positively, which can change negative behaviors to positive behaviors, and 3) they motivate one to do positive deeds. So a man thinketh, so is he. This thought asserts the importance of self. The way that you think about yourself will determine how you view your life and the world around you.

Affirmations can assist with positive thinking and also give you a positive worldview. When should you recite affirmations? Set aside time, about 10 minutes each day, to recite your affirmations. Below, are the pretty girl affirmations that I created. Say these daily, along with your own affirmations. Speak life in the atmosphere with these affirmations.

PRETTY GIRL AFFIRMATIONS

I. I affirm that my prayers are penetrating heaven and God is responding to my prayers. My spiritual walk with God is the most sacred area of my being. God is with me and he shall lead and guide me into all truth. There's purpose for my life. My steps are ordered by God.

II. I affirm that my mind is at ease. Depression, anxiety, stress, or any form of psychological bondages cannot reside in my mind. I affirm that I have peace. I think on things that are good, lovely, and are of good report. I think, therefore I am. I believe that something good is about to happen.

III. I affirm that all of my body systems are functioning properly. Disease cannot reside in my temple. I am free of all illnesses, infirmities, and diseases. I affirm that I will exercise, eat healthier foods, and take care of my body on a consistent basis.

IV. I affirm that my relationships, both platonic and romantic are healthy and reciprocal. I affirm that all forms of toxicity in my relationships will be removed. Every unproductive association will be removed from my life. I will honor and respect all healthy and covenant relationships. I will use proper conflict resolution skills when necessary. I will express the love of God to those whom he has placed in my life.

V. I affirm that I will never be broke another day of my life. I affirm that my bank account with multiply exponentially. I affirm that I will use the appropriate measures to become and maintain debt free. I am the lender and not the borrower. I affirm that my name is associated with wealth.

VI. I affirm that I will embrace my sexuality, as God has created me to be a sexual being. However, within the confounds of covenant does God honor sex. For single women: I will wait while God prepares me for my Boaz. Until that time, I will remain chaste while also learning about pleasing my potential mate. For the married women: I will please my husband and honor my marital bed. I will not withhold sex from my spouse because of anger. I affirm that we will have a healthy sex life.

VII. I affirm that I will exude the grace and class of a woman. I will maintain proper decorum, grooming, and etiquette.

CHAPTER 9: PRAYER STRATAGEMS

A stratagem is a plan used to outwit an opponent or achieve an end. Prayer is one of the many stratagems that you can use to defeat the adversary. You have an adversary. His name is Satan. He has 3 main objectives: to steal, to kill, and to destroy. Satan, or the father of lies and pride, has had time to study you. Over the years, he has sent out darts to take you out. You must however, learn the art of spiritual warfare and use prayer stratagems to defeat the enemy.

In the art of spiritual war, you must study your opponent in order to win the war. Your opponent, Satan, is the father of lies and deception. He tries to entice you with sin and false words. He gives you suggestions that are in direct conflict with the word of God.

After you have studied the enemy, you must develop prayer stratagems to conquer Satan and the kingdom of darkness.

What are some examples of prayer stratagems?

1. Praying in your heavenly language is a prayer strategy. It confuses the enemy. When you pray in your heavenly language, your spirit man has direct divine dialogue with God and the enemy and his imps can't understand your spiritual verbiage.

2. Praying during your assigned prayer watch is another

prayer stratagem. When you consistently pray as a watchman on the wall, you gage war against the adversary.

3. Praying the scriptures is another prayer stratagem. When your prayers are in direct correlation of the Holy Writ, it serves as a shield against the enemy in the realm of the spirit. The word is life. When you pray the word, you release life in the heavenlies.

4. Being consistent and persistent in prayer is another prayer stratagem. Praying one time will not be effective. You must be consistent and persistent in prayer. If your prayers are to avail much, it is going to take a fervent prayer lifestyle. Prayers must be a daily commitment. When you are persistent and consistent in prayer, the enemy's plots, plans, and darts are immediately sent back to him in the realm of the spirit. You want your prayers to penetrate heaven and its going to take persistence and consistency in prayer.

5. Using a prayer guide or journal is another prayer stratagem. When you have a blueprint of what to pray for, you can immediately pray for the respective petition. God will not have you to be ignorant to the devices of the enemy. When you look at your journal or prayer guide, you can immediately wage war in prayer for the corresponding issues or needs.

6. Corporate prayer is also a prayer stratagem. Where 2 or 3 are gathered together in God's name, there He is

in the midst. There is power in unity. 1 can put a thousand to flight, but 2 can put 10 thousand to flight. Corporate prayer is a weapon that shoots out several darts against the adversary in the realm of the spirit. Demonic portals that were once open began to close, subsequent to corporate penetrating prayers. Demons flee because of corporate prayer. The plots of the enemy are aborted during corporate prayer.

The aforementioned, were just a few prayer stratagems. As you grow in prayer, the Holy Spirit will give you more stratagems to defeat the enemy.

Spiritual warfare is an important construct to understand as a believer of Christ. Spiritual warfare is the act of engaging in war against Satan, through the channel of prayer and other spiritual weapons. To have a clearer view of the spiritual weapons that God has given you, refer to Ephesians chapter 6, located in the bible. God has called you to fight the good fight of faith. You are a soldier in the Lord's army. Use the artillery or prayer to shoot the enemy of your soul down. Continue to fight. You shall win the war.

CHAPTER 10: PRAYER JOURNAL

A prayer journal is a visual tool that includes a culmination of prayers, corresponding prayer dates, and accompanying scriptures. You may use a prayer journal to reflect on how God has answered your prayers. It also is a measuring tool that may be used to assess the growth of your prayer life. You may place your prayer requests, petitions, and supplications in your prayer journal. Also, you may place the date when God answers your prayer in the prayer journal, coupled with the respective prayer watch. Your prayer journal is sacred and for your own records. It should be between you and God.

The following table is a specially designed prayer journal just for you. You may record and write in your prayer journal to keep record of your prayer journey. If you need to, you may refer back to the prior chapters of this book to help you with completing your prayer journal for the respective day.

PRAYER JOURNAL

Date	Type of Prayer	Prayer Watch	Prayer Request/Petition

PRAYER JOURNAL

Date	Type of Prayer	Prayer Watch	Prayer Request/Petition

PRAYER JOURNAL

Date	Type of Prayer	Prayer Watch	Prayer Request/Petition

ABOUT THE AUTHOR

Beyond the petite frame, is a prolific power packed orator. Dr. Tamarrah possesses a Bachelor's and Masters' degree in the discipline of psychology from Florida A & M University and a PhD in Christian Counseling from Northwestern Theological. She has over 15 years of educational and clinical experience in the arena of counseling. Dr. Tamarrah is the CEO of Pretty Girl World LLC, an organization that promotes wellness, empowerment, and wholeness in women. Dr. Tamarrah is the author of the cookbook entitled "Pretty Girls Cook," the producer of the DVD "Behind the Veil of Closed Doors," the producer of the DVD entitled "The Art of Christian Meditation," and the producer of the workout DVD entitled "Pretty Girls Workout." Tamarrah has a been featured on WCTV for her cooking tutorials. She has been featured of Preach the Word Network, The Greg Davis Show, Atlanta Live TV, featured as the cover of Fresh Oil Magazine, and has been featured in Tallahassee Woman Magazine. Tamarrah's passion is to empower women to become their best selves.

To find out more about Dr. Tamarrah Tarver, visit www.prettygirlworld.co.

www.ingramcontent.com/pod-product-compliance
Lightning Source LLC
Chambersburg PA
CBHW061046110426
42740CB00049B/2483